THE STORY
of
GURU NANAK

by

MALA SINGH

Hemkunt

© Hemkunt Press 1969
First Published 1969
Eighteenth Impression 2012

ISBN 81-7010-160-3

My grandmother once said to me, "If you want to remember me after I am gone, write a book on Guru Nanak so that children all over the world may know the life of a man who loved God by loving His creatures." This little book is in the memory of my grandmother Lady Raj Malik who died on 26th of September, 1959.

—*Mala Singh*

Books in this Series

Stories About the Sikh Traditions

The Story of Guru Nanak

Life Story of Guru Nanak

Life Story of Guru Gobind Singh

Hemkunt Press

401, Ansals Imperial Tower, C-Block Community Centre,
Naraina Vihar, New Delhi-110 028
Tel.: 91-11-2577-5349, 4141-2083
Fax : 91-11-4540-4165
E-mail: hemkuntpress@gmail.com
Website : www.hemkuntpublishers.com

CONTENTS

NANAK : The Day-Dreamer

"What have I done to deserve such a son!" Kalu asked in despair. "I have sent him to the best teachers in the village but he refuses to learn. I put him to work, but he does no work; all he does is day-dream. Who will take the load off my old shoulders? Cursed is my life to be burdened with a son such as Nanak!"

"You are much too hard on the boy," his wife replied, "there is a lot of good in him. His teachers are pleased with him and have been amazed at his intelligence."

Kalu was too upset to listen. "That is not very surprising for, after all, we are Vedis and Vedis are so named because of their knowledge of the holy books, the Vedas. But, as you well know, we are passing through difficult times. Our kings change every other day. Robbers loot caravans in broad day-light. Trade has almost ceased. It is becoming more and more difficult to make enough money to live comfortably. I want Nanak to be independent and earn a living for himself," said Kalu.

5

"I understand all that," replied his wife trying to soothe him, "but do not be so harsh with the boy. He is still very young. I am sure he will turn out well. Perhaps he will even be a great man. Don't you remember what our neighbour told us about Nanak when he was a little boy; about seeing Nanak asleep on the grass with a large cobra watching over him and shading him from the sun with its hood! That, as you know, is supposed to be a sign of greatness."

"I do not believe in that kind of nonsense," Kalu said angrily. "In any case how will that bring

6

money to fill our bellies? Now look at our daughter Nanaki! She is only five years older than Nanak and yet she has always been a great help in the house."

"The cobra was not all," continued his wife, ignoring her husband's interruption. "You know very well what the village chieftain said. He was riding by his fields at noon one day, when he saw Nanak sleeping in the shade of a tree. On passing the same spot many hours later, he found Nanak asleep in the same place with the shadow of the tree still over him, while the shadows of all the other trees had moved with the sun. At that time even you were quite amazed".

"You do not really expect me to believe such stories?" replied Kalu with irritation.

"Well, you must be the only one in the village who does not. There was also that affair of the buffaloes eating up a farmer's crops! Don't you remember when Nanak had gone to herd cattle the other day, he fell asleep and let the buffaloes stray on to a neighbour's field. The man was furious, he threatened to beat Nanak

if he ever let the buffaloes stray on his field again. You were also very angry with him. 'Go and see,' Nanak said to the people who had gathered, 'nothing has been damaged'. When they arrived there, not one blade of grass had been touched. The neighbours have been talking about it for weeks. You see, because of our son, God had blessed the field."

"These are just old wives' tales," Kalu retorted, "and besides Nanak has no business to be sleeping while out herding buffaloes. This just proves what I have been saying all along. He is a lazy good-for-nothing who spends all his day dreaming instead of working".

The Questioning Years

Thus the years went by and Nanak spent more and more time alone in his dream-world. He would go for long walks in the nearby forest and watch brightly coloured birds flying from branch to branch. He saw trees burst into blossom in spring, lose their leaves and flowers as the heat of the summer came on and again turn into a rich green as the monsoon broke. He would sit for hours listening to the murmur of bees on hot, still days and the shrill screams of the peacocks during the rainy season. At night he lay awake gazing at the stars—the misty cluster of the Milky Way, the guiding light of the North Star and the breath-taking wonder of meteors that shot across the sky.

He would not play with boys of his own age but preferred to listen to his servant Mardana sing songs in praise of God. He spent days in the company of holy men who came to his village. He would sit at their feet for hours, asking them about the things that puzzled him. Why did the sun rise and set? Who made the

moon and the stars? Why was man born? Where did he go when he died?

He was troubled by the differences between him and some other boys of the village. His parents forbade him to play with the sweeper's son because "he is low-born and unclean" they said. He was not allowed to go and eat with the neighbour's son because "he is a Muslim" his parents explained. Nanak was hurt because he liked to play and eat with his friends without bothering who their parents were. Why couldn't he treat all his playmates as his brothers? Did not the great God make both Hindu and Muslim, sweeper and Brahmin, men of both high and low caste? Thus he spent many hours trying to find answers to these questions and some way out of the unhappiness that surrounded him.

The Sacred Thread

When Nanak was nine years old, the family priest came to put the *Janeu*, or sacred thread, on him. Nanak was curious, "Why are you putting this thread around me?" he asked.

The priest, who was very learned and fond of children, replied gently, "The custom of wearing a *Janeu* has been passed down over thousands of years from ancient Hindu religion. Only the higher castes are allowed to wear it. It will make you a better person. And unless you wear it, you will not go to heaven".

Nanak thought for a moment and then said, "Anyone can wear this thread. There is nothing to prevent even robbers and murderers from doing so. Besides, this thread could get lost, it could break, get dirty or be burned. I should have thought it was more important to speak the truth, be good and kind, and control all evil thoughts. Only these could make a person a better man and fit to go to heaven".

Friends and neighbours who had gathered for the ceremony were amazed at his words. "This is surely no ordinary child," they all said. "He will be a great man and our village Talwandi will become famous in the world."

Nanak Gets Married

The years passed and Nanak showed no signs of changing. Then one day Kalu returned home smiling happily. His wife, surprised by his unusual appearance, asked, "What has happened? Have you won a fortune? Why do you look so happy?"

"Well," Kalu replied, looking very pleased with himself, "Our worries should soon be over. I have found a wife for Nanak. A family will soon give him a sense of responsibility."

"But he is only twelve," his wife protested.

"So what!" Kalu replied, "Was not Nanaki married when she was thirteen? That is not unusual amongst our people. Of course his wife will not come to live with him until they are both a few years older."

So Nanak was married to Sulakhni. And when he was nineteen, she came to live with him. For some time they were very happy and Nanak took an interest in household affairs. They had two sons. But this way of life did not last long.

Nanak became restless again. And soon he was spending his time, as he had always done, wandering in the woods, sitting alone for hours lost in thought or asking questions from anyone who was said to be learned and wise.

Kalu was more than ever worried about Nanak's future. He tried to interest him in various occupations by which he might earn a living. He first tried to make him a farmer. At sunrise every day Nanak was sent off to the fields. But somehow the blue sky and the drifting clouds diverted him and, in a few hours, he would be lost in contemplation in the shade of the largest tree. After a particularly severe scolding, Nanak made a special effort to look after his cattle. But the orange, green and blue butterflies which flitted from flower to flower, and the calling of the cuckoo from the mango groves, distracted his attention, and soon he was lost in his thoughts: 'Who gave the butterflies their beautiful colours? Where did the cuckoo learn its song? Why did it sing?' His cattle strayed on to a neighbour's field, whose patience had already worn thin. "Kalu," the neighbour threatened, "you are my friend. But if ever I see Nanak's buffaloes in my fields again, I shall beat him and keep the cattle".

The Boy who Traded Money for a Blessing

Kalu, tired of all these complaints, said to his wife, "Perhaps Nanak is just not interested in farming. Perhaps he will do better in trade. I shall give him money to go and buy spices and he can then go to the next town and sell them there at a profit."

So Nanak set off with the money his father gave him saying to himself, "At last I shall be able to please my father and make him proud of me. I shall go to the market and look for the shops where I can buy the cheapest goods, and my father will be amazed at my cleverness". But he had only gone a short distance when he met some holy men. They were very thin and their ribs were sticking out. They told Nanak that they had not eaten for many days. Nanak thought, "Surely these good men need the money more than my father or I do," and without any hesitation he gave them all he had.

When he returned home, Kalu asked him, "Where are the spices you went to buy? Have you

sold them already? Did you make a lot of money?"

Nanak told his father what he had done with the money.

"I gave you money to trade, not to throw away to beggars," raged Kalu.

"They were men of God, not beggars," replied Nanak, "and they were hungry. I made an excellent bargain; for those few rupees I earned their blessings. What better trade can there be?" he asked.

Kalu could no longer control his anger. He began to beat the boy. Nanak's sister, who was visiting her parents at the time, tried to plead on his behalf, but Kalu refused to hear any good of him. Seeing how annoyed and irritated Kalu had become, Nanaki said, "Let me take Nanak with me to Sultanpur. I am sure my husband will be able to find him work. We are both very fond of Nanak; he will be happy with us."

"You can take him where you like," snapped Kalu. "I have done my best and failed. I wash my hands of him."

So Nanak left his wife to look after their children and set out with his sister for Sultanpur.

All Men are Brothers

Nanak lived with his sister at Sultanpur. Her husband found him a job as an accountant to the local chief. Nanak worked very hard. He seldom made a mistake. Everyone was very pleased with the change in him. He earned the respect and affection of the chief and they became firm friends.

Although Nanak seemed absorbed in his work, every now and then he would lose himself in his thoughts. He began to write poems about the beautiful things he saw, and in praise of God who made them. He often thought of his home and remembered the happy times he had spent singing hymns with his servant Mardana. "I shall ask Mardana to come to Sultanpur and we can sing together as we did at home," Nanak decided. He wrote home to Talwandi, and a few days later Mardana came to Sultanpur.

Thereafter Nanak started to lead a strictly disciplined life. Early each morning, long before dawn, he rose and went to the river Bein, to

bathe. He sat in silence under the stars thinking of God and His wonderful world. Sometimes he put his thoughts in verse. Then, as dawn broke and the birds began to sing, Mardana joined him and they sang hymns together which Nanak had written. Many men and women came to listen to them. In the evening they sang hymns again, and shared their evening meal with anyone who wanted to join them.

Nevertheless Nanak's mind remained troubled. He was happy with his employer, who was a good man and very kind to him. But whenever Nanak praised the chief of Sultanpur, people whispered in his ear, "Yes, he is a good man, but you cannot be friends because he is a Muslim. How can Hindus and Muslims be friends!" they demanded. The Muslims went to their mosque and faced Mecca to say their prayers. The Hindus, on the other hand, went to the temple and worshipped many gods. The Hindus said the cow was sacred; but the Muslims killed the cow and ate it. Muslims insisted that all men were equal, while the Hindus said that even the shadow of a low-caste sweeper could make a high-caste Brahmin unclean.

Nanak argued with the people, "Both Hindus and Muslims believe in God," he said. "These are only different ways of showing love for God." Nanak went on to explain that these differences had caused much hate and bitterness, and many bloody battles had been fought over the years between Hindus and Muslims. "It is time, people learned to look upon God as their father and upon each other as brothers," Nanak said.

The Man who was Re-born

One day, when Nanak had gone down to the river to bathe, he disappeared. People found his clothes lying on the bank, but no sign of him. Everyone thought he had been drowned. They searched the river in vain. There was great mourning. Nanak was missing for three days and three nights. But on the fourth day, he re-appeared. People asked him where he had been, but Nanak said not a word. One day passed. Then the next day when they asked him again and again, Nanak spoke : "There is no Hindu, there is no Musalman." Those were the only words he spoke.

Everyone looked puzzled. "What do you mean?" they said. "You are a Hindu and we are Hindus. Our chief is a Musalman and your Mardana is a Musalman. How can you say there is no Hindu, there is no Musalman?"

Nanak explained. "Both Hindus and Muslims believe in God. Both worship and pray to Him. Both say that men should be good,

truthful and kind. The only difference is that they say these things in different ways. This causes a lot of misery and unhappiness. I want the people to be happy. Hindus and Muslims are the same. They should act like brothers and love each other."

Nanak gave away all his belongings. He took Mardana with him and the two set off to tell the truth to the people. Later a third man, a Hindu peasant called Bala, joined them. The three of them went preaching from one village to another. Where-ever they went, Nanak wore a strange garb. He wore clothes that were worn by holy men of both the Hindu and Muslim faith. People were puzzled by this, and asked, "Art thou a Hindu or a Muslim?" Then Nanak would explain his message to them.

Nanak put all his ideas about God into poetry, so that people could memorise them. Then he, Bala and Mardana sang them together. Soon all over the Punjab, people were singing Nanak's hymns about the One God, who is greater than anyone else, who is good and loves his creatures.

Nanak on the Holy Ganga

Nanak's first journey was towards the east. On the way he visited many holy places of the Hindus. He stayed amongst the people and saw the way they lived and worshipped. Whenever he disagreed with them, he argued gently and showed them that they were wrong.

One day, while Nanak was at Hardwar, he saw a large crowd bathing in the river Ganga. Some people were throwing water towards the sun.

"What are you doing?" Nanak asked them.

"We are offering water to our ancestors," they replied.

"Where are your ancestors?" Nanak asked again.

"Many millions and billions of miles away," the people replied.

"But will the water get there?" he asked them.

"Our holy books tell us it will," they answered.

On hearing this, Nanak turned in the opposite direction and started throwing up handfuls of water.

The people were bewildered by this and asked, "What are you doing?"

Nanak replied, "I have a farm in the Punjab which is always dry ; I am watering it."

Everyone began to laugh. "How do you think the water will reach your land in the Punjab which is hundreds of miles from here?" they asked.

Then Nanak retorted, "Your ancestors are even farther away and yet you say that the water you are throwing will reach them. Why should not this water reach my farm which is so much nearer?" He continued, "You can only honour the memory of your dead by doing good deeds. In this way you truly magnify their name."

The people looked at Nanak with respect. "He is quite right," they murmured amongst themselves. "He must be a great man."

Life by Good Deeds

On his travels, Nanak met many holy men. They had given up the society of men and lived alone in forests and caves. They said they were devoted to God and tried to prove this in various ways. Some refused to eat till they were almost dead with hunger, others stood on one leg until it was swollen with pain and the other leg was a shrivelled stick. Some buried, themselves alive for days, without air or food or water; while others went about almost naked, exposing their

bodies to the heat of the sun and the cold of winter nights. Nanak even met a *yogi* who always kept his ears and eyes closed : "By doing this I can think about God without anything disturbing me," he explained.

Nanak spent many hours thinking about the

different ways these
men had of showing
their love for God.
After much thought
he concluded that
they were misguided.
"How can fasting or
making the body
suffer prove a man's
love for God, or
make him kind and
truthful?" Nanak
asked. "And surely,

in order to do good for people, one has to live
with them and not all alone in forests and caves."
Nanak finally decided he would live amongst the
people. Then he could teach them the right way
to love God.

Gold cannot be taken to Heaven

After his journey to the east, Nanak returned to the Punjab. He stayed at home for a short while and then went to Lahore, the capital city.

One day a very rich man named Dunni Chand asked Nanak to come and dine with him. After the meal Dunni Chand asked, "Is there anything I can do for you? I am very wealthy and should be glad to grant you a favour."

Nanak thought for a minute and then pulled out a needle from his pocket. "I should be grateful if you would give me this needle when we meet in the next world after we are dead," he said.

Dunni Chand looked at Nanak with surprise. "But how can I take a needle to the next world?" he asked.

Then Nanak replied, "If such a small thing as a needle cannot be taken to the next world, how do you think you will take all your riches?

Only good deeds go with you when you die.
Money is worthless unless it can be used for the
good of other people".

Dunni Chand realised the wisdom of
Nanak's words. He gave away all he possessed and
spent the rest of his life helping the poor.

A King pays Homage to Nanak

While Nanak was in the Punjab talking and arguing with the people about God and how they could best show their love and devotion for Him, a Mughal chief, Babar, invaded India. He brought a large army of Turks who burnt the crops, destroyed homes, and killed men, women and children by the thousands. There was misery and unhappiness everywhere.

The people saw all their plans for the future destroyed before their eyes, lost hope and said, "It is fate. God must have willed this on us for our many sins. We cannot do anything about it." Nanak, on hearing them, replied, "You cannot blame God for your misfortunes, you must never give up hope. You must try and start afresh and build your future again." And whenever Nanak saw the people in despair he would repeat encouragingly "With your own hands make your own future."

It was about this time that an officer of Babar captured the town where Nanak was

staying and imprisoned everyone. Nanak and Mardana were among those taken prisoner. Everyone was put in chains and made to grind corn. In the evening Nanak began to say his prayers as was his custom. The people warned him, "If you stop grinding corn even for a minute, the guards will have you whipped." Nanak paid no attention to them and continued to pray. It is said that while Nanak was lost in prayer the wheel of the mill continued turning on its own.

Babar's heart was touched and he ordered that all the prisoners should be set free and their property given back to them. He said, "If I had known that this city contained such holy men I would never have harmed it."

The Rich Man
and the
Poor Carpenter

Once on his journeys, Nanak happened to come to a large city. He was a little tired and decided to spend a few days there. A poor carpenter, Lalo, who was known to be good and kind, asked Nanak to stay with him. A few days later a very wealthy man, Malik Bhago, who belonged to the highest Hindu caste, gave an enormous feast and invited Nanak to be his guest. It was considered a great honour to be asked to dine with a man as rich and powerful as Malik Bhago. Over a hundred people went to the feast. But Nanak did not go. Malik Bhago noticed Nanak's absence and went to see him the next day. "You eat the coarse bread of a poor, low-caste carpenter," he said, "and yet you insult me by refusing to come to my feast. However I have brought some specially prepared cake for you".

Nanak did not reply. He took the cake from the man. He asked the poor carpenter to

41

bring him some bread from the kitchen. Then he held the rich man's specially prepared cake in one hand, and the poor, low-caste carpenter's bread in the other, and squeezed them. From Lalo's bread flowed milk and from Malik Bhago's cake there poured a stream of blood. Malik Bhago looked horrified. "Why is there blood coming from my cake and milk from Lalo's coarse bread?" he asked.

"Lalo's bread was earned by honest hard work. But your cake and the riches you have collected have all been gained by robbing and cheating the poor," Nanak replied.

Malik Bhago admitted that Nanak had spoken justly. He felt ashamed of his evil deeds. Thus Nanak changed yet another man from his sinful ways to a life devoted to helping the poor and needy.

There is only One God

While Nanak was travelling over the countryside, he often saw people praying before stone images of gods and goddesses. They put the idols to bed at night, woke them in the morning, dressed them in silks, and gave them food to eat. They firmly believed that these idols had the power of granting them all their wishes and of making them rich and happy. "If we serve them in this way, our gods will be pleased with us," the people said, "and they will surely reward us."

Nanak tried to show them that their ways of worshipping God were wrong. He questioned them, "You say you are good Hindus. Yet all you do is go to the temple once a day and burn incense before a stone image. The rest of the day you lie, and cheat and steal. Why should God be pleased with you?"

The people thought for a moment about what Nanak had said, and then replied, "You are right. But our fathers, and their fathers before them, taught us that this is the  right way of showing our love for God. Everyone else considers us to be good Hindus because we respect our gods and honour them by taking them out in procession on festivals and by arranging feasts for them".

"You are like children, not sure of what is right and what is wrong," Nanak told them. "You should ask the advice and guidance of a teacher, a guru. He will help you whenever you are in doubt. All men have goodness in them; but as the sunflower only opens to the rays of the sun, so men need a guru to open up the goodness that is in their hearts and show them the way to God."

Then they all gathered round Nanak and asked him, "If we have been in the wrong, you tell us the right way of worshipping God."

"You know that there is only one God," Nanak replied. "He made everything—he made you and me and everyone else. He made the flowers, the birds and the trees. You should pray to God often, wherever you are, and repeat His name. But prayer alone is not enough. You should cleanse your mind of all unkind thoughts. Help people in distress, work hard and give some of your earnings to the poor."

Thus, wherever Nanak went, he converted large numbers by his teachings. These people became his disciples and called themselves Sikhs. To this day the followers of Nanak are known as Sikhs.

Sajjan the Robber

There lived a famous robber called Sajjan. He was as cunning a man as he was cruel. He built a temple full of gods and goddesses for the Hindus and a mosque for the Muslims. "This will lure both Hindus and Muslims to my house," he said to himself, "and, at night, when they are asleep I shall steal all their money and jewels and then kill them."

One day Nanak was passing nearby and decided to spend the night at Sajjan's house. Sajjan welcomed him warmly and spread out a great feast of tasty dishes before him. But all the time he was thinking, "This man, Nanak, looks very happy and content. He must be very rich. Tonight I will rob him of all his money and then murder him. No one will know anything about it."

At sunset Sajjan began to urge Nanak to go to bed early. "It is getting late and you look tired," he said in a voice full of concern for his guest.

Nanak answered that he always sang a hymn before retiring for the night. Sajjan was getting impatient but he agreed to sit down for a few minutes and listen to Nanak. Nanak sang a song he had composed himself :

> *Herons and birds of prey are*
> *found in holy places*
> *Yet they eat living things ;*
> *They are beautiful*
> *Yet their hearts are evil.*

Sajjan realised that what Nanak said about herons and hawks applied to him too.

"What Nanak says is quite true," he admitted to himself. "I might appear kind and friendly, but I am like these birds Nanak speaks of. Although I do not eat people I do almost the same thing, for I kill them". He fell down at Nanak's feet and asked his forgiveness.

Nanak said, "Sajjan, only God can forgive you. And God only forgives those who admit their sins openly and repair the wrongs they have done. Tell me how many people have you robbed and killed?"

Sajjan looked very ashamed. "I have murdered and robbed many hundreds of men, women and children. How would I possibly obtain God's forgiveness for all my evil deeds?"

"Give away all you have gained in this way to the poor," Nanak said.

Sajjan did as Nanak had asked and became his follower. The first Sikh temple in India was built by Sajjan the robber, in gratitude to Nanak who had changed his way of life.

God is Everywhere

Nanak's last journey was towards the west. He wanted to go and see the places which Muslims considered holy. So he joined a band of pilgrims on their way to Mecca.

One day, during the journey, he fell asleep in the mosque. Suddenly he was shaken awake. Standing above him, glaring down at him furiously, was a *Mullah*, the Muslim priest of the mosque.

"What do you think you are doing?" the *Mullah* demanded angrily. "Have you no respect for religion? Why are you sleeping with your feet towards Mecca which is the house of God?"

Nanak replied gently, "If I have made a mistake, please correct me. Turn my feet to where there is no God".

The *Mullah* was taken aback. "You know that you should always face Mecca," he said. "Even our dead are buried with their faces towards Mecca."

Nanak replied, "But God is everywhere. Your own holy book the Koran says 'whichever way you turn, there is the face of Allah'."

On hearing such wisdom the *Mullah* fell down at Nanak's feet in admiration and asked Nanak to forgive him.

After this, Nanak went to Mecca and from there to Medina and westwards on to Baghdad. Everywhere he met people who believed firmly that they were very religious and devoted to God.

"It is obvious that we love God," they told Nanak whenever he questioned them. "We observe our yearly fast, we go on pilgrimages and we pray five times a day".

"Yes, you do all these things," Nanak gently scolded them, "but you forget to be honest, kind and generous. Giving one rupee to a poor, hungry child is more important to God than hundred prayers. Being truthful is of greater value than a thousand fasts. Kindness and consideration please God more than any number of pilgrimages."

In this way Nanak won the hearts of many Muslims.

God Made all Men

Nanak returned to the Punjab after many months. He wished to end his days in the countryside he knew and loved best. So he settled down with his family at a small town named Kartarpur.

One question kept troubling him, "Are not all men equal? Why then is the Brahmin regarded as holier than the sweeper? Surely this division of man from man is inhuman?" Nanak often said.

So he decided to try and change the system which by building walls between men caused such bitterness.

"I will make sure that any men or women who come to me, be they rich or poor, of high caste or low, shall eat together. They shall take it in turn to cook and wash the dishes. For why should only the Brahmin be considered clean enough to cook?" Nanak said, "And moreover all shall recite prayers. Then we shall have no priests who can look down on other men."

Large numbers of people began to gather to see Nanak and hear him speak of God. Nanak told them how they should live. He asked them to wake up three hours before sunrise, bathe in the stream and then go to the temple to recite the morning prayers and sing hymns. Thereafter they were to be free to earn their living. In the evening after having done a full day's work, be it farming, shop-keeping or weaving, the people were asked to gather to pray and sing hymns. After this they all dined together in the temple. Before going to bed to sleep, everyone was expected to say another short prayer.

This became the life of work and prayer of Nanak's followers all over the country.

Nanak Chooses a Successor

As Nanak grew older, he began to look around for someone who could carry on the work he had started. He did not think either of his two sons fit for the job. His elder son, Sri Chand, had become a hermit. He lived alone in the forest, praying and fasting. "How can a man guide people, if he cuts himself away and goes and prays alone in the forest," Nanak always said. Nanak's younger son, Lakshmi Das, was the exact opposite. He was only interested in making money. So who could Nanak choose as his successor?

Among his followers, Nanak was very impressed by a man called Lehna, who had repeatedly proved his great devotion to God. Nanak changed Lehna's name to Angad which means 'of my own body' and told him to spread his message and set an example for all.

The years went swiftly by and Nanak was now approaching 70. With old age he became frail, but his interest in the world around did

not wane. The woodlands in flower, the mustard in bloom and the calling of the *Papeeha* as the monsoon broke, still sent him into poetic rapture.

Nor did his love for the people lessen with the years. He was never too tired to listen to their problems and was always ready to offer words of comfort and advice. The circle of people who respected him and followed his guidance increased daily.

There is never enough of Goodness

People often ask, "What did Nanak do which was so unusual?" He himself admitted that he was not a special messenger of God and could perform no miracles except reciting the name of God. He was just a teacher like so many others. And India is full of teachers and holy men.

Nanak answers this when he tells of an incident at Multan, during his travels. A local priest came up to him and presented him with a cup of milk, filled to the brim, saying, "This city is already full of holy men. We have no room for nor need of anyone else."

Nanak plucked a petal from a jasmine flower and put it in the cup, where it floated on the milk and scented it.

"There is always room for holiness and goodness," Nanak answered. "Just as one jasmine petal can perfume a whole bowlful of milk so can one man re-fill the world with the fragrance of faith in God and in good deeds."

The Holy Man
of the
Hindus and the Muslims

Nanak realized that he had not long to live. As the hour of his death drew near, the Hindus and the Muslims gathered at his bedside began to cry.

Nanak tried to comfort them. "Why are you sad?" he asked. "We are all born and we must all die. I just want you all to pray for me".

There was silence in the room. But soon the sound of murmuring disturbed Nanak. The Hindus and the Muslims were quarrelling bitterly amongst themselves.

The Muslims said, "We will bury him. It is the custom among our people".

"No," replied the Hindus. "We will burn his body. That is the custom among our people".

Nanak then spoke, "Why do you argue needlessly? You can place flowers on either side,

Hindus on my right, Muslims on my left. Those whose flowers remain fresh tomorrow can do as they wish with my body".

Then Nanak again asked both Hindus and Muslims to pray. They prayed all night. Before the sun had risen, Nanak was dead. But the flowers on the right and left of him were fresh.

To this day, about 530 years later, Nanak is remembered by millions of followers whom he brought together by his teachings of love and brotherhood. How could India forget the greatest of the holy men, the Guru of the Hindus and the Pir of the Muslims!

Nanak's Prayer

There is One God.

He is the supreme truth.

He, the Creator,

Is without fear and without hate.

He, the Omnipresent,

Pervades the universe.

He is not born,

Nor does He die to be born again.

By His grace shalt thou worship Him.

Before time itself

There was truth.

When time began to run its course

He was the truth.

Even now, He is the truth

And evermore shall truth prevail.